ASK AN EXPERT
CLIMATE CHANGE

Richard Spilsbury

Published 2009 by
A & C Black Publishers Ltd.
36 Soho Square, London, W1D 3QY
www.acblack.com

ISBN HB 978-1-4081-0853-6
     PB 978-1-4081-1300-4

Series consultant: Gill Matthews

This book is produced using paper that is made from wood grown in managed, sustainable forests. It is natural, renewable and recyclable. The logging and manufacturing processes conform to the environmental regulations of the country of origin.

Produced for A & C Black by Calcium.
Printed and bound in China by C&C Offset Printing Co.

All the internet addresses given in this book were correct at the time of going to press. The author and publishers regret any inconvenience caused if addresses have changed or sites have ceased to exist, but can accept no responsibility for any such changes.

Acknowledgements
The publishers would like to thank the following for their kind permission to reproduce their photographs:
Cover: Creatas: Joel Simon; Shutterstock: EGD, Robert Adrian Hillman.
Pages: Dreamstime: Robert Byron 21t, Flynt 20; Istockphoto: Brasil2 11bl; Rex Features: K Nomachi 17t; Shutterstock: Melissa Brandes 15, Andrzej Gibasiewicz 13, Mike Graham 19, Eray Haciosmanoglu 9, Robert Adrian Hillman 16, Nik Niklz 12c, Gregory Pelt 18t, Melissa Schalke 5, Robert St-Coeur 7bl, Donald R. Swartz 14b, Vera Tomankova 8c, Peter Wey 10t. **Illustrations:** Istockphoto: John Bloor; Geoff Ward.

Contents

What is Climate?

Meteorologists or weather scientists, like me, study the **climate**. Climate is the pattern of weather each year.

Weather patterns

I live in the UK. The pattern of weather there means that autumn is windy and winter is cold and snowy. Spring is rainy and summer is hot. In other places on Earth the climate stays the same all year round. For example, deserts are always very dry.

This map shows the types of weather in different places around the world.

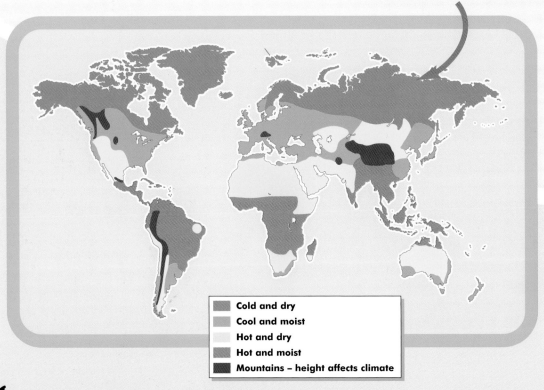

- Cold and dry
- Cool and moist
- Hot and dry
- Hot and moist
- Mountains – height affects climate

Climate change

You might be surprised to know that world climates haven't always been the same. We know this from finding clues. For example, scientists found ancient tree trunks in rock beneath the thick Antarctic ice. This clue proves that climate was once warm enough in Antarctica for forests to grow there.

Climates changed slowly over thousands or even millions of years. Meteorologists think that climate change is much faster now.

The Antarctic ice of today covers land where trees once grew.

How Does the Earth Stay Warm?

The Earth stays warm because of the **greenhouse effect**. Greenhouses trap the sun's heat inside. The temperature is then warmer inside than outside. My tomatoes become red and ripe faster in my greenhouse because it is so warm.

Sun

Trapped heat

Atmosphere

Trapping heat

The Earth's **atmosphere** acts just like glass in a greenhouse. The atmosphere is a mixture of gases. Sunlight shines through the atmosphere. Some of the sunlight heats our planet's surface but most bounces back towards space. Some of this heat then gets trapped and stored by gases in the atmosphere.

The greenhouse effect controls the temperature on Earth.

Warm enough to survive

Most living things need to stay warm to survive. Without the greenhouse effect the whole Earth would be as cold as Antarctica.

Living in cold places

Animals in cold places have special features to keep them warm. For example, whales and seals are very fat to survive in cold water. Many other living things that don't have these features could not survive in the freezing temperatures.

This seal's fat is about 10 cm (4 in) thick. It can survive in temperatures as low as -45°C (-49°F).

0°
-10°
-20°
-30°
-40°

Is the Greenhouse Effect Increasing?

People are changing the atmosphere by producing **greenhouse gases**, including **carbon dioxide (CO_2)**. These gases cause the greenhouse effect. We release carbon dioxide by burning **fuels** such as coal, oil, and gas in machines. Engines in cars, aeroplanes, and other vehicles use fuel to make them move along.

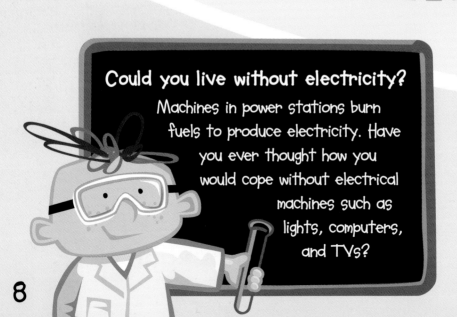

Power stations release greenhouse gases from chimneys.

Could you live without electricity?

Machines in power stations burn fuels to produce electricity. Have you ever thought how you would cope without electrical machines such as lights, computers, and TVs?

Carbon dioxide changes

In the past, the amount of carbon dioxide gas in the atmosphere stayed about the same. Living things, including people, give off carbon dioxide when they breathe out. Green plants use the gas to make their food.

Today, the extra carbon dioxide that machines release is building up in the atmosphere. It builds up faster than plants can use it. It is storing even more heat and increasing the greenhouse effect.

Gases from aeroplane engines increase the greenhouse effect high in the sky.

9

Is the Earth Getting Hotter?

The greenhouse effect is getting stronger so the Earth is getting hotter. Weather fans like me have noticed that the average temperature on Earth each year has risen a little.

Tree blossom appears earlier because winters are warmer.

Rising temperatures

The average temperature on Earth is rising. The years between 1996 and 2008 were the warmest since 1850. We call this **global warming**. There are other signs of this global warming, too, such as changing seasons.

Heating up

I like sunny days but very hot, dry weather for days on end can be dangerous. People become exhausted and sick. Very young and very old people who are weak may even die from heatstroke.

In other places the heat causes forest fires. The fires spread fast through the trees because leaves, branches, and trunks are so dry.

There is a danger of forest fires when the temperature reaches 35°C (95°F).

What is Happening to the Arctic Ice?

Global warming is making the **Arctic** ice melt. During the long Arctic winter, the ocean surface around the North Pole is frozen into a layer of floating ice. Some of this ice melts during the short Arctic summer.

Nothing to eat

In recent years, warmer seawater has melted far more sea ice than usual. Polar bears roam across this sea ice to find seals to eat. However, when the ice cap shrinks, the seals move away. With no seals to hunt, polar bears can starve.

Polar bears eat up to 9 kg (20 lb) of meat each day!

Looking for food

Polar bears prefer to eat seals, and sometimes berries or reindeer. But when polar bears are hungry, they sometimes wander into Arctic towns and villages to find food.

Sinking in soil

Land in the Arctic, such as Greenland, is usually buried under hundreds of metres of ice. The ice formed from frozen, piled up snow. Because of global warming, Greenland ice is thinner. It is even disappearing in some areas. The Arctic soil that normally stays frozen solid all year round is also melting. This means that houses and roads built on the surface sink into the soft soil.

The Arctic ice is disappearing so fast there might be none left by 2050.

Are the Oceans Rising?

Climate change is making the **sea level** gradually rise. Sea level is the height of the top of the oceans. It is rising partly because there is more water in the oceans. Another reason is that warm seawater takes up more space than cold seawater.

Melting ice

Global warming is making ice melt at the Arctic, Antarctic, and on cold mountain tops. The extra water is gradually filling up the oceans, rather like when we put more water in a bath.

11 of the world's 15 largest cities are built on coasts.

Life on the coasts

Many people around the world live along coasts. When the sea level rises seawater slowly spreads across coastal land. People's houses may then flood. Some people have to move away because there is less land to live on.

Seawater soaks into the soil. It spoils underground drinking water supplies. It also makes fields too salty to grow crops.

Buildings in coastal towns and cities can be covered with water when flooding occurs.

What is a Drought?

In summer there is so little rain that I have
to water my plants. A drought is when there
is almost no rain for months on end. Climate
change is causing more droughts in drier parts
of the Earth, such as Australia. During a drought,
rivers, lakes, **reservoirs**, and wells run dry. This is
because they are not topped up with rainwater.

Soil that is too dry in
fields cracks, crumbles,
and blows away
in the wind.

The effects of droughts

Wet places, such as marshes, dry up during
a drought. Plants and animals there may die.
People have less water to drink and wash with.
Farmers may not have enough water to give their
farm animals or put on crops. Tens of millions
of people are affected by
drought each year.

When people cannot
grow enough food
for themselves
or their animals,
many go hungry.

Suffering because of drought
People in poor countries suffer more
than those in rich countries in a
drought. This is because they
have less money to buy
water or food.

Will There Be Stormier Weather?

I've been talking to lots of other meteorologists lately. We agree that storms are getting more powerful. These storms damage or flatten homes, schools, and other buildings. They can blow sharp objects around that injure people.

Climate change

Stormier weather is caused by climate change. That's because big differences in air and water temperatures between some areas are making violent winds and storms blow.

Violent storms blow down trees and damage houses.

World's worst storms
The worst storms are called **hurricanes** and **tornadoes**. During tornadoes, winds can travel faster than a Formula 1 car.

Landslides and floods

Sometimes the heavy rainfall during storms soaks into the soil. On slopes the wet soil may slide down. The **landslide** can bury houses. Sometimes floods happen because water cannot soak into the land or get carried away in rivers. People and animals can drown in floods. Sometimes roads and bridges are washed away.

Dirty water

Flood water washes dirt from land and from **sewers** into drinking water. People get sick if they do not have enough clean water to drink.

Cars and the people in them can quickly become trapped in a flood.

How Can We Help the Climate?

You might be surprised to know that you can slow climate change. All you have to do is look after the atmosphere. This means producing fewer greenhouse gases.

Power choices

Different countries around the world are starting to make more electricity without burning fuels. Instead they use the wind, rushing water, or sunlight to make power. However, we can all choose to use less power as well.

Wind turbines make power from moving air without burning fuel.

20

Power saving tips

The most obvious way to produce fewer greenhouse gases is by taking fewer trips in vehicles that use fuel. Many families share cars and take fewer foreign aeroplane trips to save fuel.

Cycling to school uses no fuel.

Remember:

- 💡 Turn off lights when you leave a room
- 💡 Don't leave computers or TVs on standby
- 💡 Use low-energy light bulbs and washing machines
- 💡 Cycle or walk to school with friends
- 💡 Buy recycled goods – many take less power to make than new goods

21

Glossary

Arctic cold region around the Earth's North Pole

atmosphere layer of air surrounding the Earth

carbon dioxide (CO_2) type of gas in the atmosphere produced when living things breathe out and also when burning fuels

climate average, normal pattern of weather through the year

fuels substances, such as coal, that we burn or use up in other ways to release heat

global warming general rise in temperatures worldwide

greenhouse effect when gases in the atmosphere trap warmth from the sun, warming the Earth

greenhouse gases gases that absorb heat

hurricane powerful spinning wind creating storms over warm oceans

landslide movement of soil or rock down a steep slope, often triggered by rainfall or an earthquake

meteorologists scientists who study the weather and climate

reservoirs large stores of water that are used by people

sea level average height of the ocean surface

sewers network of pipes used to carry wastewater from toilets, sinks, showers, baths, and laundry

tornado powerful storm with a vertical tunnel of wind

Further Information

Websites

The United States Environmental Protection Agency has created some excellent animations of how the greenhouse effect works at:

http://epa.gov/climatechange/kids

Visit the Encyclopedia of the Atmospheric Environment to learn about climate, weather, and acid rain at:

www.ace.mmu.ac.uk/eae/english.html

Find out about rising sea level, the problems for polar bears, and check out the Climate Change News at:

www.coolkidsforacoolclimate.com/Causes&Effects/ RisingSeaWorld.htm

Books

Global Warming (Protect our Planet) by Angela Royston. Heinemann (2008).

Weird Weather: Everything You Didn't Want to Know about Climate Change, But Probably Should Find Out by Kate Evans and George Monbiot. Groundwood Books (2007).

A Hot Planet Needs Cool Kids: Understanding Climate Change and What You Can Do about It by Julie Hall. Groundwood Books (2008).

Understanding Global Warming with Max Axiom, Super Scientist by Agnieszka Biskup. Capstone Press (2007).

Index